THE ONLY
WORLD BUILDING
WORKBOOK
YOU'LL EVER NEED

Compiled by

For project

Name of this world / location / society

Series Bibles for
Writers

T.M. HOLLADAY

"The Only World Building Workbook You'll Ever Need"

First published by Naniloa Books, 2020

Copyright © 2020 Series Bibles for Writers

Authored by T.M. Holladay

First edition.

My fellow writers,

World building for fiction is absolutely vital. And I'm not just talking about fantasy and other speculative fiction. Whether you are writing a story set in history, in an alternate reality, in the future, or in the here and now, you need to understand the world in which your characters live in. Their world shapes their daily lives. Their geography, government, and culture spawns the obstacles that come their way. The more you know about where your characters live, the more immersive the experience can be for your readers.

The following pages contain questions and prompts to help you flesh out your setting. Not all questions will pertain to your world, and that's okay. You'll probably leave some questions or even whole sections unanswered. This workbook is meant to help creators in all genres, which will mean some areas are more important to some writers than others.

Before you get started, might I suggest that you give a cursory read through of the questions first. This will not only get your creativity going, but it will help you spread out your data into the appropriate places instead of trying to cram too much info into one answer box. Also, as you fill out one page, it might inspire insight into previous pages. And on that note, you certainly don't have to go through this book front to back in order. *Insider tip: have this book spiral bound at your local printer for an even smoother experience!

Though the probing questions herein can inspire leaps in creativity, be sure to do your appropriate research. Make sure your geography answers fit within the type of biome(s) of your setting. Make sure your military responses make sense with the type of government chosen. Make sure your culture and foods and labor distribution work with the resources of the area. Readers can be quick to call out things that don't make sense, so don't be the author that has pineapple-moose kabobs as the staple food of a desert-dwelling nomadic people.

There are extra pages for notes or sketches in many sections of this book. Feel free to draw maps, floor plans, clothing, weapons, vehicles, flags, athletic fields, or whatever else comes to mind as you explore this new world you're creating. (Or the historical world you're discovering!) You can always attached printed images to these pages as well.

Here's to welcoming your readers into a world that feels so real, so legitimate, they'll feel like their own character in your story. I'm genuinely excited for you! Create something we'll never forget. This book will be here to keep all of that incredible data organized. And though you won't explain all of this information to your reader in unnecessary descriptions, info dumps, and unnatural dialogue, (you really, really shouldn't), the fact that you as the creator knows this world so well will manifest in how your characters behave, how the world around them reacts, and how your plot unfolds.

So have at it, folks. Make something incredible.

TM Holladay

"I'm not going to tell you how to start a bug-powered vehicle, I'm just going to put you inside one with someboy who knows how, and send you off on a ride."

— Kameron Hurley, Lightspeed Magazine, October 2013

THE NATURAL WORLD 7

Biomes	8
Geography	9
Weather	10
Time	11
(Maps)	12
	13
	14
	15
	16
	17
	18
	19
	20
	21

RESOURCES & ECONOMY 22

Resources	23
Resource prompts	24
Economy prompts	25
	26
	27

HISTORY 28

History prompts	29
(History & lore)	30
	31
	32
	33
	34
	35

GOVERNMENT & POLITICS 36

Government	37
Lines of succession	39

Law & justice	40
Foreign relations	41
Military & War	42
(Battle maps & borders)	43
	44
	45
	46
	47

FAMILY 48

Family structure & culture	49
(Family trees)	50
	51
	52
	53
	54
	55
	56
	57

DIVERSITY 58

Class distinctions	59
Diversity	60
(Groups, clans, races)	61
	62
	63
	64
	65
	66
	67

LABOR & INDUSTRY 68

Industries, jobs, positions	69
Labor questions & class distinctions	70
(Uniforms & markers)	71
	72

73

74

75

SOCIAL EXPECTATIONS — 76

Morals, ethics, & values — 77

Social expectations — 78

79

80

81

RELIGION — 82

Religious foundations — 83

Creation story — 84

Religious rituals & holidays — 85

Religious symbols — 86

88

89

LANGUAGE & COMMUNICATION — 90

Communication — 91

Language — 92

(Codes, alphabets, & notes) — 93

94

95

TECHNOLOGY — 96

Technology — 97

(Descr. & sketches) — 98

99

100

101

EDUCATION — 102

Education — 103

104

105

HEALTH — 106

Health & wellness — 107

108

109

FOOD — 110

Food & drink — 111

Culinary culture — 112

113

APPEARANCE — 114

Beauty & hygiene — 115

Special occasions — 116

(Sketches) — 117

118

119

120

121

122

123

124

125

STRUCTURES — 126

Utilities & public works — 127

Buildings & structures — 128

(Blueprints & sketches) — 129

130

131

132

133

134

135

136

137

ARTS & ENTERTAINMENT
138

Art & culture 139

Sports, pastimes, & hobbies 140

141

142

143

MAGIC
144

Magic system 145

Magical beings 146

Magical things 147

148

149

150

151

GROUP LISTS
152

153

154

155

156

157

158

159

NOTES
160

160

161

162

THE PHYSICAL WORLD

"It's a spiral into madness. I think, 'He's going to need to spend some time in a really big city. Industrial revolution Londonish.' Where do big cities happen? At a confluence of trade routes. That's influenced by rivers. Where do rivers come from? There's aquifers and stuff. I ask these questions. I go 'Why, why, why, why, why?'"

— Patrick Rothfuss, on where he begins his world building.

Desert

Very little rainfall and water sources, though prone to infrequent, intense rainstorms that cause flooding. Specialized vegetation and animal life. Not very many deserts have larger mammals, instead they host reptiles, vertebrates, insects, and oftentimes birds and small mammals. There are four major types of desert biomes: hot & dry, semi-arid, coastal, and cold.

Grassland (Temperate)

Trees and large shrubs are absent. (North American prairie, Mongolian steppe) Hot summers and cold winters, with moderate rainfall. Seasonal drought and occasional fires are very important to biodiversity. Very fertile soil, though droughts, fires, and large grazing animals prevent bush and tree growth. Much of this biome has been converted to farmland.

Savanna

Grassland with scattered individual trees, always found in warm or hot climates. Rainfall is concentrated in 6-8 months of the year, followed by a long period of drought when fires can occur. These fires are not devastating to the ecosystem, but rather support it. If the rain were well distributed throughout the year, savannas would become tropical forest. Porous, rapid-drain soil.

Forest

Characterized by well-defined seasons with a distinct winter. Moderate climate and a growing season. Precipitation distributed evenly throughout year. Soil is fertile, enriched with decaying litter. Canopy is moderate and allows light to penetrate, resulting in well-developed and diversified vegetation and animals. Broad-leafed trees that lose their leaves in the winter.

Tropical Forest (Jungle)

Greatest diversity of species. Occur near the equator. Only two seasons (rainy and dry). The length of daylight is 12 hours and varies little. Average temperatures do not vary by more than 5 degrees year round. Nutrient-poor, acidic soil. Tall upper canopies deeply shade the forest floors, where the shallow roots of the trees mingle with ferns, mosses, palms, and vines.

Taiga (Boreal forests)

Characterized by very low temperatures. Long, cold, dry winters and short, moist summers. (Alaska, Canada, Scandinavia, Siberia). Soil is nutrient poor and acidic. Canopy is dense with low light penetration, leading to a limited understory. Evergreen trees with needle-like leaves. Extensive logging.

Tundra

The coldest of all the biomes. Treeless plains, frosted landscapes, extremely low temperatures, little precipitation, poor nutrients, and short growing seasons. Low biotic diversity. Limited drainage, simple vegetation, and large animal population oscillations because of migration and hibernation. 2 types: Arctic tundra, and high altitude mountain tundra.

Mountains

Mountain regions can be found in many biomes (desert, tundra, forest, etc.) Important to note what altitude does to temperatures and biotic adaptations. (Only certain plant life can handle higher altitudes. Animal life has also adapted.) Usually unsuitable for farming.

Freshwater

Rivers, lakes, and streams, often rich with nutrients swept in from rainfall and snow melt. Supports the surrounding animal life. Rivers attract population settlements because of transportation and water.

Estuaries

Where freshwater streams or rivers merge with the ocean. Nutrients and salinity mixes, creating very interesting, adapted ecosystems. Deltas can both create and solve problems of population settlement.

Marine Shallows

Oceans contain the richest diversity of species. Intertidal zones include beaches & tides. Coral reefs found in warm, shallow waters, often as barriers to continents and islands. Pelagic zone (the open ocean) is generally cold, though experiences a constant mixing of cold and warm currents. Abundant sea life, from large mammals to plankton.

Deeper Ocean & Abyss

Benthic zone grows colder in its depths and contains sand, silt, and dead organisms. Nutrient rich, which leads to abundant fauna. The Abyss (deepest canyons and parts of the ocean) is very cold and highly pressurized. Tectonic plate ridges, hydrothermal vents, and chemosynthetic bacteria, which feeds the many invertebrates and fishes.

Sky / Atmospheric

Consider the the chemical makeup of the atmosphere (nitrogen, oxygen, argon, carbon dioxide) and its other particles, such as water vapor, dust, pollen, pollution, and plant grains. Consider temperatures, weather, storms, wind currents, ionospheres, UV and solar flare protection, and gravity.

Space

Consider temperatures, space storms, light, and zero-gravity. Consider magnetic fields, electromagnetic radiation, cosmic rays, and the vacuum of low density particles. Think about what objects or formations are nearby. (Space dust, space junk, planets, asteroids, space stations, suns, moons, black holes, galaxies, etc.) How near is near?

Consider the smaller ecosystems of your world.

Reefs, volcanoes, other planets, moons, atolls, oasis, valleys, canyons, islands, kelp forests, meadows, swamps, highlands, nuclear fallout zones, cave systems, deltas, ice fields, lakes, streams, rocky shores, etc. Research their flora and fauna. The benefits, the resources, the dangers, the protections. Add your smaller ecosystem(s) here:

Describe the biome in more depth. (Details significant to world development that aren't mentioned on the previous page.)

Does the story take place on Earth? If so, where? If not, where?

Are the laws of nature and physics the same as our Earth?

Are there multiple biomes in the primary setting? Describe.

Are there outside biomes or regions mentioned? What natural biomes border this one?

What is the size and scope of the setting? How much of it is inhabitable?

Bodies of water:

Significant natural formations such as valleys, hills, ridges, caves, reefs, dry river beds, canyons, deltas, sinkholes, volcanoes, etc.

Have the activities and development of the inhabitants affected the climate or geography?

Is the region difficult to travel? Is there travel between the inhabitants and outsiders?

Describe summer.

Describe autumn / fall.

Describe winter.

Describe spring.

If your world does not have these four seasons, describe the seasons it does have.
(i.e. If your story takes place underwater, the seasons might be classified with the changing currents.)

What do storms look like?

Are there natural disasters that are expected and prepared for?

What natural forces are most feared?

What natural forces are most desired?

What does the sky look like during the day? Cloud formations? Pollution? Moons? Space junk? Fog?

What does the sky look like at night? Moons? Light pollution? Constellations? Comets? Space junk?

What point in time or history does this story take place? (Historical years, or vague eras, or alternative history, or the future, etc)

How much time does the story span?

Are there multiple timelines?

If this is an alternative history, what was the catalyst that separated the timelines? How much time has past?

Is there time travel? How does it work? (science or magic?) (Fixed timeline, dynamic timeline, or multiverse)

Does this society differentiate years / time differently? What kind of calendar?

What kind of timepieces do the residents use? Or do they judge time in a natural way?

Other info or sketches:

MAP

13

MAP 15

MAP

17

MAP

19

MAP

21

RESOURCES & ECONOMY

"Water has the potential to grow life even in the barren desert, and it also has the potential to flood an entire city destroying countless lives - fire has the potential to give heat in the freezing winter, and it also has the potential to burn an entire forest to ashes. Potential is neither good nor evil, it's our intention that makes the distinction."

— Abhijit Naskar, See No Gender

Ponder each item's source, output, health, & value, or whether such type even exists. Take note of anything noteworthy.

Water

Crops & orchards

Domestic animals

Seafood

Wildlife

Usable space

People

Shells, pearls, etc

Textiles & fibers

Papers, inks, paints

Spices, sugars

Metals

Gemstones

Minerals

Stone, clay, etc

Timber, etc

Energy or fuels

Technology

Synthetics

Medicines

Magical

Drugs, illegals

Describe the water resources, where they come from, their purity, and how individuals get it and pay for it.

What resources are available in abundance?

What resources are only accessible to the wealthy or upper class? Do those resources provide comfort? Or power?

What resources are never available, but heard of? Why?

What resources are the most used/valued by individuals in day to day life?

What resources are most valued by the government?

Do any resources change or evolve in their value? Is it a naturally occurring process, or do characters trigger the change?

What is the population? (regions, towns, nations, etc). Compare to the physical space and the available resources.

Have any resources been a reason for war?

Is there currently a population shift going on?

Type of Economic System:

Market Economy (Free Enterprise/Capitalism)	Command Economy (Socialism/Communism)
Individuals freely own and operate the factors of production. (No current world government operates this way.)	The government owns and operates the factors of production. (Cuba, China, Laos)

Traditional Economy (Agrarian Society)	Mixed Economy
Based upon customs & traditions, and hunting & agriculture. (Haiti, Chad, Rwanda)	Has features of both market and command economies, such as regulated capitalism. (USA, Great Britain, Japan)

What is used for official currency? Who mints it?

What is used for unofficial currency? Is it acceptable by the government or illegal to use?

How healthy is the state of the economy? Static, upward, or downward?

What does the distribution of wealth look like?

Describe any gambling, black markets, or risky investments, etc that goes on in this society.

How prolific is trade on the individual/family level?

Where are small trades made? Marketplaces? In secret? Outposts? In homes? Under supervision?

Is there significant trade with outsiders?

IMPORTS: (and from where)

EXPORTS: (and to where)

HISTORY

"An editor once wrote on the top of a manuscript I'd written: 'Needs more lore.' MORE LORE is the best advice I ever got."

— R. L. Stine

How far back does their known history go?

How did the society come to be? What initiated the inhabitation of this location? (geography, war, immigration, decree, etc)

Are there any big events in the past that this society still talks about?

Are there any past natural disasters that influenced the progress of the society?

Does the geography/ecology show signs, scars, or other markers of its settled history?

Are there any past and/or current wars or battles that influence the progress of the society?

How accurate is their known history? Has the government or anyone else re-written history to suit their needs or agendas?

Are there any hero/villain duos in their history that are referenced?

Where did any cultural or biological diversity come from?

How is history passed down?

GOVERNMENT & POLITICS

"World building has two parts. One is the actual creation. The other is bringing the world into your story. Everything you create should not be in your story. You will create parts of your world–coinage, magic, religion–that you're especially proud of. And because you made it, you want to tell someone about it, because we are storytelling creatures. But most of your world building should not show up in your story. I encourage you to really ride the brake. Rule of thumb: 10 percent of what you know should be in your story. For me, it's about 4 percent."

— Patrick Rothfuss

Type of government (monarchy, republic, feudal, aristocratic, democracy, dictatorship, anarchy, oligarchy, tribal/clan/family independence)

Head of state, both their title and their real name.

Is there a more powerful force behind-the-scenes or is the face of the government also the most powerful?

Explain the line of succession. (Public vote, secret vote, a predestined heir, series of takeovers / coups, a competition, or some other process?)

What is the support system for the leader(s) called? (advisors, court, counsellors, cabinet, etc). Discuss roles, authority, and how they're appointed. You can list all members of this support system on the "list" pages in the back of this workbook.

Is there a system in place to balance/check the highest ruler? The government as a whole? Does that system actually work?

What services does the government provide? (schools, defense, water access, justice, utilities, rations, etc)

How is the government funded? Taxes? Voluntary tribute? Is this system stabilizing or hurting the society?

How and when did this current government come to into power? (War, religion, peace, treaty, slow development over time, or some other way?)

How stable is the government? Peaceful? Volatile? In transition? Explain.

What is its biggest weakness?

What is its biggest strength?

Does the government monitor its citizens? Is there a census, license, or registry system? Who is considered a citizen?

Discuss any story-pertinent political alliances.

Are there political sides, parties, or opponents?

Are there any groups or people that have particular influence on the government without actually being employed in government?

Does the protagonist have a voice in the government? Does the villain / antagonist?

What is considered conservative? Liberal? What are the most controversial issues?

How are borders marked? Walls, oral history, mountain ridges, rivers, electrical fields, etc. Mark them on the maps in the Physical World section.

What effect have the geography and the resources had on the creation and stability of the government?

Does diversity play a role in the government? Are there excluded demographics?

Does magic play a role in the government?

How influential are the religious leaders in government? How influential are they in the political opinions of the people?

Other:

Use this space to map out the historical and expected future lines of succession for the rulers of this society.

List the rights given to the citizens of this society, especially those that will pertain to your story.

List any notable laws and rules, especially those that will pertain to your story.

How are laws created? How are laws revoked or changed?

Explain this world's concept of justice and of proving one innocent or proving one guilty.

Who gathers evidence and/or intelligence? Are there rules that regulate them? Are they the same people that make the arrests?

How does the court system work? Does it apply to everyone? Are there separate civil and criminal courts?

Explain typical punishments for lawbreakers, especially for the laws listed at the top of this page.

Are personal weapons allowed? Which ones? Is there a regulation system for these? Are certain demographics excluded from personal weapons?

Are there any groups of people that do not have the same rights as others? Why?

Are there ambassadors to outsiders? Who are they? Who picks them? Explain roles and authority.

Is foreign policy influenced by political marriages and/or progeny?

Is it common for average citizens to come into contact with foreigners? Or are foreigners a novelty? Or are they only spoken of, but never seen?

Does the tone of the relationship between merchants of this nation and merchants of other nations mirror the tone of formal political relationships?

How informed is the general public on the status of their society's formal relationships with outsiders?

Describe the current relationships as they stand with various outsiders, whether tribes, cities, nations, or worlds.

How quickly can relationships with outsiders turn? Are alliances easily and quickly broken? Are there circumstances in which enemies can quickly become allies? Or are relations between nations or societies deep rooted, reliable, and difficult to change? Provide examples.

Is there a military? What are they called? Who do they answer to? Who pays for them?

Is the military centralized? Or loosely structured like a militia or national guard?

Are people drafted or volunteered into the army? Explain the process and expectations.

Is it integrated? (genders, ethnicities, species, etc)

Are there currently any ongoing wars? Describe their name, cause, purpose, and short history. (More room to explain on later pages.)

Is war supported on the homefront? Why and in what ways?

What is the proportion of professional soldiers versus untrained recruits?

How and where are troops trained?

Does social status play into military rank? Must one buy an officer commision? Or is rank determined by seniority? By skill? Is there rank / title mobility?

Can military rankings / knighthoods occur during battle or must they wait for formal occasions?

What weapons of war are available? What armor?

How are troops transferred, fed, and housed?

How does intelligence gathering work? How much time does it take and how accurate is it? How is secret intelligence communicated?

Use this space to map out possible battles or other war boundaries and histories

Use this space to map out possible battles or other war boundaries and histories

Use this space to map out possible battles or other war boundaries and histories

FAMILY

"Social dynamic theory is philosophy, not politics. There can't be only one correct answer, or there would only be one book."

— Sharon L Reddy

What do typical families look like?

How is procreation viewed? Do the government or religious leaders encourage or discourage childbirth in any marked way?

Are there any customs, superstitions, punishments, and/or celebrations surrounding the birth of a child?

Expected male gender roles:

Expected female gender roles:

Expected childhood roles:

Expected elderly roles: Also, what does society do with the aging elderly?

Are marriages valued? Are they a result of courting, convenience, law, business, or are they arranged? Also, are marriages considered a religious institution or civil arrangement?

What do children call their parents? Vice versa?

How is homosexuality viewed? What about transgendered people?

How important is lineage in this society? How important is it to the protagonist?

DIVERSITY

"If you're worldbuilding, don't rely on stereotypes. Noble savages and white heroes and damsels-in-distress and people of a single race acting in a single way. No culture is monolithic, skin color does not determine demeanor or magical racial bonuses, men are not all one thing and women are not all another thing. Stereotypes are lazy at best, harmful at worst."

— Chuck Wendig, Terribleminds

Consider the class system that may or may not exist in this world. Compare that to the class distinctions throughout world history: France's Bourgeoisie vs. the Proletariat; the European system of class and titles; the ancient Roman Patricians vs. Plebeians; the modern world's Upper, Middle, and Lower classes; etc. Describe your world's classes below. Consider including the highest elite (royals, heads of state, goddesses on earth...), upper, middle, lower, and if this world has any of the lowest of classes (the "untouchables").

NAMES and brief DESCRIPTIONS of social classes. (write or sketch) (there are blank mini profiles on the following pages for your use as well)

Are their ranks / titles? List their hierarchy

Is movement between social classes encouraged? Why?

Is movement between social classes hard? Why?

Are marriages between social classes common?

Does social class affect life span, immunity, or health in a notable way?

What do residents look like? Is there a dominant ethnicity or species, and if so, describe their general appearance.

Briefly explain notable biological diversities that exist. (species differences, unexpected coloring, stature differences, powers/magical differences if they are passed down because of biological lineage, malformations, etc) There are blank mini profiles in the following pages. Please note, the third workbook in this series, "The Only Fantasy Workbook You'll Ever Need," contains many pages for race/species comprehensive profiles.

Are any of these differences treated with injustice, contempt, or other negativity?

Are any of these differences revered or valued? Or considered exotic in a good way?

Do any of these differences affect social class? Jobs? Where they can live?

Does anyone fight to correct the injustice of misunderstood diversity?

Explain any notable non-biological diversities that exist. (religion, political affiliations, body or medical alterations, etc)

Are there any notable markers that flag or otherwise indicate someone's differences? (such as gay-pride rainbow pins, special tattoos, Freemason rings, or the Star of David patches in Nazi Germany WWII,) Are these natural, chosen, or forced upon?

Are there any differences (biological and/or non-biological) that can be changed via extreme measures? (surgeries, dangerous initiations, etc.)

GROUPS, CLANS, RACES, SPECIES

LABOR & INDUSTRY

"When a reader enters the first chapter of your book, they're trying to get their bearings. It's our job as authors to give them the signals they need in order to be able to navigate that world."

— Leigh Bardugo, on World-Building and Having Faith in Your Abilities (Writers Digest)

(Remember your world's geography, ecology, and resources.)

Agricultural

Industrial

Public service (government employed) and utilities

Military, warriors

Enforcers (police, investigators, monitors / auditors)

Educational

Household help or servitude

Medical and health

Creative arts and entertainment

Transportation, travel, and hospitality

Religious and/or symbolic

Trade, business, market

Construction or other hard labor

Natural resources, mining, etc.

Information & communication

Illegal, black market, or otherwise clandestine work

Are there group(s) or industries (i.e. military) large enough to require the participation of most family units? Which, and why?

Are there group(s) or industries available only to a certain family or genetic/magical subset? Which, and why?

How are vocations/careers chosen?

Are there any careers notable in your story that require specialized training or apprenticeships? For how long?
While in training, how are they and their skills viewed by society?

Which (if any) jobs require uniforms? (pages to sketch or describe uniforms are provided on the following pages)

LABOR DISTRIBUTION AMONG THE CLASSES

LOWER CLASS	MIDDLE CLASS	UPPER CLASS

SOCIAL
EXPECTATIONS

"Just as small details matter, so do the small interactions of
our characters. The way one shares her food. The way another
addresses a superior."

— Chuck Wendig, Terribleminds

As a whole, where do this society's ethics come from? Religion? Paternal/maternal tradition? The law? Inner choice? Survival?

In this society, which is the most acceptable choice: **honoring your parents/family or obeying your ruler?** Explain why.

In this society, which is the most acceptable choice: **helping the many, or helping the few at the expense of the many?** Explain why.

In this society, which is the most acceptable choice: **death, or survival with shame?** Explain why.

What is the hierarchy of duty? What or who are people expected to honor most?

Who are the rebels and why? How are they socially dealt with?

What things are considered offensive or shocking in this culture that aren't offensive in yours? What are society's reactions to those things?

What things are considered normal that are taboo, shocking, or offensive in your own culture?

Is any form of slavery going on in this society?

What is this society's views on the treatment of animals?

List any notable hierarchies in this society's values. Where might these comparisons stem from? (Integrity, loyalty, honesty, courage, power, money, honor, land/property, equality, intelligence, wisdom, status, love, justice, influence, fame, creativity, compassion, beauty, achievement...)

Rules to be observed between authorities and non-authorities:

Rules to be observed between classes:

Rules to be observed between genders:

Notable insulting behavior or gestures:

Notable admirable/honorable behavior or gestures:

How does a host behave? How does a guest behave?

How much time is afforded in daily life for social situations?

How do couples court? Does it change between clans, groups, species, or classes?

HOW TO GREET SOMEONE

STRANGERS	FRIENDS	SUPERIORS / ELDERS	INFERIORS / YOUNGERS	OPPOSITE GENDERS

Other greetings between other types:

How are names shared / said? Suffixes? Titles? Is where you're from part of your name? Are there reasons for names to be secret?

RELIGION

"Every world has religion and myths to explain its creation and how it will eventually end. The only difference is, when it's your story's world, you get to choose!"

— Kathy Edens, ProWritingAid

Name of dominant religion(s):

Monotheism, ditheism, polytheism, atheism, deism, animism, henotheism, or dystheism?

How big of a role does faith play in the everyday lives of citizens?

Is your protagonist religious?

Do they believe in life before life?

Do they believe in life after death?

Do they believe in a creation story? (room to write out the story in full detail on the following pages)

Is religion's role in your story positive, neutral, negative, or "it's complicated"?

Does religion affect the economy? Does the economy affect religion?

Does the ecology / geography affect the religion?

Is magic involved in their religion?

Is the church controlled / influenced by the state?

Are there any god(s) that directly interact with the inhabitants?

Are there churches, cathedrals, temples, shrines, and/or other places of worship?

Do religious relics, artifacts, art, or symbols appear in **homes?**

Do religious relics, artifacts, art, or symbols appear in **public spaces?**

Are there religious rituals and/or traditions? Explain. (Who, what, where, when, why)

Describe the religious holiday(s).

Do any holidays require or encourage travel? How much of the population is able to travel for this holiday?

What do weddings look like?

What do funerals look like?

Describe any rites-of-passage, whether religious or not.

LANGUAGE & COMMUNICATION

"Rapid communication should always be considered during the world building phase of a story. Even something as basic as Game of Thrones' ravens, which function like feathered text messages, would have drastic consequences."

— Oren Ashkenazi, Mythcreants

How do people express joy?

How do people express reverence and/or respect?

How do people express frustration and/or anger?

How do people express love?

How are oaths or promises made?

How widespread is literacy?

How is information shared among the masses? (news, radio, town-cryer, scribes, word-of-mouth, personal tech devices, etc)

How are messages shared/sent between individuals?

Are there any secret or magical devices for communication?

Other:

What is the official language(s)?

What other languages are spoken? By whom?

Are there multiple dialects? Spoken by whom? How does speech differ by demographic?

What is the language most likely to be understood among both residents and foreigners? Why?

Are there any secret languages or codes? (Record secret codes, alphabets, or languages on the following pages)

Does it make sense for your characters and society to have some of the same idioms, phrases, and slang that you currently use?

Unique or foreign phrases:

TECHNOLOGY

"Many authors make the mistake of treating tech like confetti. They toss as much as possible into a story without doing the work to develop it. This often bogs down the narrative with terms and devices that don't really do much for the plot. My advice is to focus your story on a few key discoveries."

— Rachel Somer, Be Your Own Mentor

Sources of energy: (light/solar, electric, burning fuels [gas, coal, or wood], nuclear, magic, wind, hydro, or chemical reactions.)

Does their current understanding of technology surpass the tech of their past? Or is it behind from the technology of their past? If it is behind, why? How does this society's technology compare to our current real-life tech?

How accessible is technology to the masses?

Does technology play a role in their communication?

Does technology play a role in their medical progress?

Does technology play a role in weapons and military?

Is technology used in transportation?

Is technology an export? An import?

Types of tools available to laborers:

Is there anything recently invented that could upset the balance of power?

EDUCATION

"A writer can create a more just world in books by shining a light on that injustice."

— Yang Huang

Who has access to formal education?

Do they get to choose what to study?

Are there different types of education / schools / apprenticeships / etc? Or are all students educated in the same manner?

At what age do children begin their formal education? When are they finished?

How much of the population has access to advanced education? (i.e. university) Is it expensive?

How easy is access to information? Books, internet, libraries, etc.

Does the society place enough value in education that the technology of their world continues to advance?

How valued are educators?

HEALTH

"What they wear, what they eat, what they drink, what they value, what they want, this is all worldbuilding and it goes on until the last page of the story.."

— Scott Lynch, interview at WorldCon, 2017

Describe the healthcare system. (Centralized? Person-to-person? In-home? Requires travel? etc.)

Describe the healthcare professionals. Healers? Doctors? Medicine women? Healer robots? How accurate is their medical knowledge and skills?

How are healers trained? Are they regulated?

How affordable is it to seek medical attention?

Are there enough healers for the level of sickness in this world?

Does the lifestyle of the average resident contribute to good health?

Does magic play a role in healthcare and wellness?

Are available medicines natural/herbal in nature? Or chemical/synthetic in nature? Both?

What is used for antiseptic?

What is used to dull pain?

FOOD
& CULINARY
CULTURE

"I like to wonder what people would have for breakfast—
which people, as their breakfasts would be different—and
where they would get those food items, and whether or not
they would say a prayer over them, and how they would pay
for them, and what they would wear during that meal, and, if
cooked, how ... Breakfast can take you quite far."

— Margaret Attwood

As you ponder this section, remember the geography and resources. Think about proteins, fats/oils, grains, and produce.

Typical meals for the lower classes:

Typical meals for the middles classes:

Typical meals for the upper classes:

Typical meals for the rulers and/or highest elite:

Are there processed and/or packaged foods? Industrialized food?

How is food cooked? Who cooks?

How is food preserved? How is it stored in homes?

How available is food? Stores? Marketplaces? Self-sufficient homes? Rations?

Is obesity common? Is famine or starvation common?

DRINKS

Is drinkable water readily available? Is it free?

Are there alcohols or other mind-altering drinks?

Hot drinks? Sweet drinks? Milks?

When do people eat? How often?

Are there public places to eat?

Are the culinary arts valued? How does someone show appreciation for a meal?

Does society value family "sit-down" meals?

Describe the items used during a meal. The table, utensils, seating arrangements, etc.

Do any foods or recipes provide special abilities or magic?

When food is scarce, who gets priority? (The laborers who produce, the children, the revered elderly, the military, or the nobility?)

Are meals used for courting, dating, or other social activities or rituals?

Are there any special foods, recipes, or culinary customs for particular holidays?

Are there other particular culinary traditions? Religious? At the start or end of war? At the ascension of a new ruler?

APPEARANCE

"The muse in charge of fantasy wears good, sensible shoes."

— Lloyd Alexander

Describe notable standards of beauty. Consider hair, cosmetics, accessories, and body image.

Describe any typical hygiene practices that differ from your own.

Is hygiene valued differently across various groups or classes?

Are there differences in clothing, hair, or appearance between married people and single people?

Differences in clothing, hair, or appearance because of puberty, a right-of-passage, or some other marker of adulthood?

Is the upper class day-to-day clothing more flamboyant, more sleek, or more subdued?

What textiles are easily available? Which ones are rare? (consider cottons, linens, silks, synthetics, hides, leather, wool, etc.)

How available or rare are certain kinds of dyes? Embellishments?

Are there things that rebels wear on purpose? Hair? Make-up?

What things are considered "old fashioned"?

How does society view modesty?

Changes in clothing/appearance for travel:

For social events:

For particular holidays:

On the battlefield:

For funerals and/or while in mourning:

For religious worship:

For weddings: (The bride, the groom, the officiator, the attendees)

What does the ruler wear during official ceremonies or duties?

Other:

STRUCTURES

"In many ways, the world you build for your tale will be a character in itself: it will have its own look, feel, sound and smell."

— Tim Hillebrant, The Writer Life

Describe the water system. Wells? Plumbing? Desalination? Canals? Delivery? Rain collection?

Describe the waste/garbage management. Public pick-up? Burning? Live in filth? Individual? Landfills? Zero-waste society?

Is there a system of electric power or other energy? How do residents light their homes at night?

Describe the sewage and/or drainage. Are there toilets?

Describe the types of infrastructure. Roads, waterways, bridges, connections, public transportation, etc.

Describe what they do with dead bodies.

Other:

Resources available for construction:

Architectural styles:

How do buildings integrate with the geography? (Stilts in a bayou? Carved from cliff sides? Stone to withstand the wind?)

Are there structures built for protection from invaders?

Are there structures built for protection from natural forces?

Are there city-centers or other areas that the masses would congregate during times of celebration or emergency?

What do the industrial centers (if any) look like?

Are there structures built for entertainment purposes?

Where is the government headquarters located and what does it look like? How accessible is it to the masses?

Other significant buildings, structures, or landmarks?

TYPICAL HOMES OF THE

LOWER CLASS	MIDDLE CLASS	UPPER CLASS

ARTS & ENTERTAINMENT

"When you get some free time, write. When you get some lazy time, plan. When you get down time, world build. When your time comes, shine!"

— Ace Antonio Hall

Are fine arts considered noble or immoral?

Are artists / performers / creators respected?

What arts are the most widespread? (painting, pottery, fashion, music, literature, photography, digital, magical arts, etc.)

Are there public showcases of the arts? (Theaters, music halls, galleries, etc.) Are they profitable? Do they have patrons?

Are there traveling, private, or temporary showcases of the arts? Are they profitable?

Is there artistry in their landscaping and architecture? Or are these areas more utilitarian?

Other:

Are there public and/or private parks and gardens?

What sports or pastimes are played? Are they formally organized or spontaneous? (Room to explain rules or sketch fields/courts on following pages.)

Do any sports require highly specialized training and/or money to participate?

What games are commonly played? Are any of them a form of gambling?

How common and/or available are books? Has the printing press been invented? Do people read for entertainment? Who are the storytellers?

Are there electronic medias available? (movies, recorded music, TV, internet, other digital text, etc.)

Are there public and/or private dances? (Ballroom parties, harvest festivals, rain dances, etc.) Are these dances used in courting?

Other:

MAGIC

"If you choose magic you will never be able to return to the life you once lived. Your world may be more ... exciting ... but it will also be more dangerous. Less reliable. And once you begin to walk the path of magic, you can never step off of it."

— Neil Gaiman, The Books Of Magic

This chapter prompts a brief, foundational overview of the magic system in your world. However, if this world has intricate magic, with multiple magical species, animals, and/or objects, or with different types of magical abilities for different characters, then we highly recommend the use of "The Only Fantasy Workbook You'll Ever Need," another workbook in this series.

Does this world have epic magic, small-time magic, or subtle magical realism?

What type of magic? (White, grey, black, natural, elemental, witchcraft, folk, voodoo, shaman, ceremonial, enochian, etc)

Where does magic come from? God(s)? Nature? Specific resources such as minerals, locations, or objects? Will power or individual life-force? Genetics?

Does magic require some sort of trigger or rite of passage, or is it gradually earned over time/training? Explain.

Who has magic and what powers do they specifically have? (can list individuals or groups).

Logistics of magic. How is it used? (words, objects, wands, ingredients, etc.)

What is the cost of using magic? Does anyone try to circumvent that cost?

What can magic NOT do?

Is the magic known among all the inhabitants, or is it kept secret? If so, how?

Is magic encouraged, forbidden, or viewed indifferently?

Are there different types or races of **magical humans**? (Wizards, vampires, shifters, people with fire magic, etc). Explain their abilities.

Are there **magical non-humanoid inhabitants**? (Aliens, gremlins, mermaids, unicorns, centaurs...) Explain their abilities.

Are there **magical animals**? Explain their abilities.

Are there **magical items and objects**? Explain their ability and purpose.

Are there **magic places**? Explain their location, purpose, and abilities.

Are there magical **foods and/or other consumables**? Explain their abilities.

EXTRAS

"One of my challenges [as a writer] is to make sure that I'm giving the reader details that the character cares about rather than details that I care about. I'd say that's key to world-building."

— Jessica Andersen

Innate purpose

Location

Time frame

Requirements

GOOD	
BAD	
NEUTRAL	

Plot
purpose or
story arc

History

LIST

	NAME / PLACE / ITEM / ETC	LABEL	DESCRIPTION
1			
2			
3			
4			
5			
6			
7			
8			
9			
10			
11			
12			
13			
14			
15			
16			
17			
18			
19			
20			
21			
22			
23			
24			
25			
26			
27			
28			
29			
30			

OTHER INFO

Innate Purpose

Location

Time frame

Requirements

	GOOD
	BAD
	NEUTRAL

Plot
Purpose or
story arc

History

LIST

	NAME / PLACE / ITEM / ETC	LABEL	DESCRIPTION
1			
2			
3			
4			
5			
6			
7			
8			
9			
10			
11			
12			
13			
14			
15			
16			
17			
18			
19			
20			
21			
22			
23			
24			
25			
26			
27			
28			
29			
30			

OTHER INFO

Innate purpose

Location

Time frame

Requirements

| GOOD |
| BAD |
| NEUTRAL |
| |

Plot
purpose or
story arc

History

	NAME / PLACE / ITEM / ETC	LABEL	DESCRIPTION
1			
2			
3			
4			
5			
6			
7			
8			
9			
10			
11			
12			
13			
14			
15			
16			
17			
18			
19			
20			
21			
22			
23			
24			
25			
26			
27			
28			
29			
30			

OTHER INFO

GROUP

Innate Purpose		GOOD
Location		BAD
Time frame		NEUTRAL
Requirements		

Plot
Purpose or
story arc

History

LIST

	NAME / PLACE / ITEM / ETC	LABEL	DESCRIPTION
1			
2			
3			
4			
5			
6			
7			
8			
9			
10			
11			
12			
13			
14			
15			
16			
17			
18			
19			
20			
21			
22			
23			
24			
25			
26			
27			
28			
29			
30			

OTHER INFO

Innate purpose	
Location	
Time frame	
Requirements	

GOOD
BAD
NEUTRAL

Plot purpose or story arc	
History	

LIST

	NAME / PLACE / ITEM / ETC	LABEL	DESCRIPTION
1			
2			
3			
4			
5			
6			
7			
8			
9			
10			
11			
12			
13			
14			
15			
16			
17			
18			
19			
20			
21			
22			
23			
24			
25			
26			
27			
28			
29			
30			

OTHER INFO

Made in the USA
Las Vegas, NV
14 August 2023

76080946R10090